COPY RIGHT PAGE

All rights reserved,

Including the right to reproduce this book or portions thereof in any form whatsoever.

For information, address

Angel Ferguson's WordProcessing

11500 of the Americas, Tampa, FL 33617

Copyright * 2016 by

Felicia McCardy

All Rights Reserved

Published in the United States by

Angel Ferguson's WordProcessing, FL

Art Work

Angel Ferguson

WWW.ANGELFERGUSONSWORDPROCESSING.COM

Printed in the United States

ISBN-13:978-0692746028 (CUSTOM)

ISBN-10:0692746021

Dedication

To all mother's, who in spite of their own families, have lent a helping hand to help a sister, friend or whomever is in need of guidance.

ADDITIONAL BOOKS BY THE AUTHOR

DON'T STARE AT ME PLEASE

PARENTS LIKE ME

A Mother's Purpose

At birth is not when it starts. It starts when we were born. To be a good mother is something that comes naturally through being mothered correctly. Sometimes there's someone else who intervenes to make the process of mothering be a experience that is mastered and passed on like grandma's recipe, you know the one that everyone wants!

As I have said many times, my mother was a strong mother, going that extra mile for her 4 children. Staying up late at night trying to figure out what to do next with her fixed income. So often at times not feeling well yet still putting in a 12 hour work schedule. Always making it look easy, as I find myself doing. It's sometimes not what we do as a mother but how we do it. My mother worked numerous jobs, for example as a driver for the school system & for a private company, she cleaned homes, always doing her best at whatever job was available to her. I didn't meet her mother (my grandmother), maybe I was to young to remember if I did but there is one thing for sure, she was more than likely a very hard working woman. Back then, there was no choice, you knew once you had a child (baby) it was your responsibility to take care of him/her. But O' how have times changed!

Regardless of how a mother is feeling, she puts her best face and attitude up front. As a mother there are many sacrifices. Now I'm sure some mother's were born with money as to where everything that child needed they could get.

Mothering can come with challenges. As a mother you have to be willing to step aside for their well being. When you have a child with a disability you must make sure to take time out for yourself. The reality is that if you are the main caregiver, you must take care of you. There are many up's and downs being a parent.

Some parents will decide at birth that it will be too much of a burden or that they are unwilling to put their lives on hold for a child. At times, I think back about the birth of my daughter. At the time, I had no idea she had a disability. It was my mother that brought it to my attention each time we went for a visit, she would say "Felicia, something is wrong with her". My response was always the same, "momma, she is ok". You see, I was told because she was born early, she would be delayed but would eventually catch up to other children her age. I remember her first birthday, she was not sitting up, yes I was concerned but I went off of what the doctor's had told me. Because my mother had raised four children, had seen more that I had, yes she was more knowledgeable than the doctors. To be honest, I never asked questions about her being disabled or when would she catch up, I just believed that the doctors knew what was best and knew it all! I knew I had to figure out if something was really wrong with her, for her sake, if for no one else.

Feb, 1988 my mother passed away, it was unexpected but somehow she prepared myself and my siblings (the one's that were still at home) She had only known my daughter Keishawn for a short while before leaving this earth.

She sent someone to bring my oldest brother from a drug hole located in Thonotosassa, FL. She prepared a large amount of food for a few days. Somehow she must have known within herself what was ahead. How and why she did this, I could never explain but once again, she was doing her motherly duties. Not long afterwards, an aunt whom lived next door said to me "I'm making an appointment with Maurice's pediatrician". I figured this Dr. would say the same but we walked into his office with me carrying Keishawn. He said hello, then said "I know the problem". Me thinking yeah right, what problem? His reply was, she has CP. I first thought CP– I was silenced for a minute not knowing what these letters meant. Therefore I asked, what is it? He answer was, she has Cerebral Palsy. Really! I remember thinking she was right. My mother, whom had recently passed was right. From that day, my journey for her began. A few doctors said if she made it passed her younger years, she would remain like a baby. My reaction was like really– God gave this baby to me. For her to do nothing, at first I was mad but at this time I had no relationship with God, yet I knew I wanted better for her. I just wanted to be the best mother. I no longer had my mother but I had stored so much from her being such a loving, devoted, hardworking woman/mother.

I loved my baby no matter what I would have never left her behind for someone else to raise even if I had of known about her disability from the beginning. As a person with a disability, I was told it's best to get them in school early. My goal was to get her walking and potty trained by August 1990, so she could be a big girl. While talking with my father's sister Linda, they told me about a place called Shriners. This placed offers services for free of charge to families like myself. So, I set up an apt and a date was set. I was told for her to walk she would need both heel cords lengthened. She would be in a cast with both legs for several months. So we did have the surgery. I thought at one period in time "this is not going to work", she was so used to being carried, she didn't want to bare weight on her feet.

After the cast's were removed a few months went by, still nothing. Than one weekend while in Clearwater, Fla, visiting a dear friend while the adults were talking and kids were playing, music and dancing I heard a little voice "Keishawn, come on you can do it". As I watched and listened I thought one day this will happen. The kids continued to dance and she, Keishawn leaned on the sofa for support. All of a sudden she took her first step.

My heart fluttered with joy. I wanted to scream but I knew if I did this may have startled her and then she may have never done this again.

That was the start of what I would call a new beginning. I had told myself I would not potty train her until she could walk. So on this day we had to rejoice. First on the inside then prepare for training. Keishawn is about to be 4 and still in diapers but that is ok, I always took it one day a time. You see as parents we have hopes and dreams for our children, yet mine were quite simple, like walking, talking and being able to go to the bathroom. As a mother, I wanted as all other mother's wanted for their child, to simply be better than me. Not to make the mistakes I made. Yes, too not have to work as hard as I say my mother did but what I started to realize is my dreams for Keishawn would be on hold for her first 5 years of life would be some what survival skills and praying a lot that each day of her life would be better. So by the age of 6, I was in a different mind set, now with her learning, saying her ABC's and 123's a breath of relief, let the dreams began that one day she may be a productive person, able to exceed to whatever she wanted to do or be. Thinking back on her first 5 years of life were some what dark. Some doctors saying she may never do much of anything. But as I think back to the dark times of her life I can't help but wonder how her life may have been if I were not her mother. But then I think everyone has a purpose but we as mothers have a special purpose. Even the doctors or even family members think of a child's situation as to be of – NO HOPE but a mother will continue on when it seems there is no hope for the situation and yes being raised by a true mother of purpose made me say so many times to myself Felicia, really God gave you this child for a purpose.

At this point in my life I really didn't have a relationship with God. My relationship with him was like most people just acting like I knew him. But here it was many years I went thru acting like I can do this by myself, after all I had been given a visual aide thru watching my mother. Thinking it was so many times I would watch my mother and say now why would she do such a thing when she has 4 children on her own, working numerous jobs to survive but she did the things she did because of her visual aide from her mother which in turn passed down to me. I'm not sure why God chooses our perfect plan. A mother's definition is not simple, sometimes we smile when we really want to cry, we stay awake when we should be asleep trying to figure out which direction to take next. We say we are okay when inside we really don't have a clue about what to do next. But then there is what's called purpose. Why we were actually created for the care of our children, so we set aside all and become determined to create a resolution to any problem which occurs and do this with the greatest determination. Did I not know what was ahead of us?

December 18, 2003 was like no other morning, got Keishawn up, prepared her for school then off we went down our regular path on Pine St., not knowing our lives were about to be changed forever. As we made it thru old Hillsborough and Pine. O how I dreaded the wait at the light and at 92 and Pine this light seemed like you sat for a good 5 mins before you would get a green light to go.

As the traffic to the left and right started to slow down I knew it was about the time for my light to turn green but as it turned green for a split second I hesitated to go then reality kicked in really quick, this light is going to change really quick so just as I started to go, I took my left and saw what looked like a train coming, I remember looking back at Keishawn in the back and saying Lord have mercy for I thought this was it. I tried to go quick and get out of the this vehicle's way because it was clear it was not stopping for it's red light, I'm guessing prior to impact I lost conciseness because the next thing I recall the conversion van we are in flipped over and I hear voices saying are you all right.

All I could say was "where is my baby (Keishawn) . My mouth was busted open and Keishawn was just laying on the side of the inside wall looking dazed. We both were assisted out the rear door by paramedics. As we were loaded in to make our trip the ER, I thought we made it. But what I did not know is at the moment of impact our lives were changed forever. *We were x-rayed and released. For weeks* I would have difficulty eating. At this time at I was employed at what I would call my dream job, had my own desk. This was all about to change in Early January 2004.

The sleepless nights, caring for Keishawn had started to take it's toll. It was like I had a new born baby not by choice. She had started getting out of the house while we were sleep, looking for herself and I know it sounds crazy but it was like she was another being trying to find some lost family. Not only this, she had returned to having to be fed. Becoming incontinent , which at the time I thought was all temporary. As weeks went by at this time taking FMLA from work, reality set in. This accident that we survived has now created a nightmare. We were at the hospital at least once a week because she wouldn't sleep. By mid Feb I was in a state of thinking "what do I do now"?

I myself had to seek counseling, feeling some days like what next, why me after all life was going so great up until Dec 18, 2003. Not only did I end up loosing my dream job, we were suppose to close on a dream home. This was not going to happen now. It took everything out of me just to survive this nightmare. So Keishawn is wearing briefs, being fed and to top it off behaviors everyday was like fighting an army so I had to do something for me to stay sane so I agreed to get on Xanax.

Yes, yes, yes. I felt so good or should I say high, not giving a care about the change in Keishawn nor the lost of my job nor my dream home. By March, her birthday I had just about said, the hell with this whole situation but I knew in order to gain control back I had to start dealing with the new life. So I stopped the Xanax and did a reality check of myself and thought this is my child, I remember taking her to that pediatric doctor and being told I could put her in a group home to get her under control. As I rode home from the office I remember thinking "finally some relief" but just as the key went in the door to go in with her yet again a reality check hit me I rushed to the phone to let the doctor know I had a change of heart. I was not getting any sleep but if someone else was taking care of her surely I would need Xanax . Once again just to deal with feeling as a failure as her mother. So as time went by, behaviors became worse but I was in it for the long haul. I had to do something for me. So because the behaviors were so bad she would not stay at school, that was a nightmare. looking on at home like "oh my God what are you going to do"?

I decided to do something, I enjoy making money, see people and just to simply get away from home. So I found a place in Brandon called Peddlers Flea Market got a booth and made the best of life (this new life). I would go to yard sales and auctions to purchase stuff to set up in my booth. I made a little area for her to sleep, watch T.V. and just do whatever. My life was starting to look up again. Money was tight but we did survive. Lots of times I would sit and wonder am I the only one going thru such a mess (tragedy of such) Also, she would end up on the floor at school and I would have to figure how to get her up first then take her back home. So it was me and her but during this time is when I found my peace with God. It was so many times I would just cry because I felt like God wasn't listening, didn't have my mother for support surely if she was still alive she would make me feel at ease. As the year went by fast and things started to settle down I thought maybe I can start working again not realizing as of yet that it would be a set back for Keishawn. In August 2004 I took a job at a place called Quest Inc., it was an eye opening experience. This place has clients that have disabilities that took my mind off Keishawn and looked as to why were there so many different disabilities. I have to say I was shocked to find I was at a place were I learned about behaviors in people with a disability was normal. I was just blessed all those years.

Taking a job was some what crazy for the first 6 months. I was late most days due to behaviors but for some reason I was now at a place were my once thought of a dream job was a thing of the past. My prior job at PMSI a mail order job that I loved so much was truly a thing of the past, my new dream job was one in which I saw myself retiring from but also giving the clients something I would want for staff to give to my daughter if ever she had to become a part of Quest or any place of such. As time when by a Dr. finally gave Keishawn a diagnosis. After months and months and years we finally had an answer. She was diagnosed with PTSD. This after almost 2 years. It was times we were out, it was like playing dodge ball when we would hear a siren. The sound would trigger behaviors. I remember one day me and my cousin and the kids were on a temp job doing Choice School ballots in Tampa, when Keishawn had a bad episode, screaming, kicking my seat due to a siren noise, I looked at my cousin and not saying anything I pulled over, yes I was angry, furious but not just at the behavior but reflecting back on the guy who hit us on Dec 18, 20003. I got out of the car (van) and started walking around it in circles a few times praying and simply saying God help us please. I remember getting in the van thru the side door, my cousin sitting in the front asking what are you going to do. Honesty I had no answer I just knew we had to make it home. I started to find anything that I could tie her hands and feet, with my cousin says "Felicia, you are going to jail", "I replied, we are playing a game". "I said Keishawn lets see if you can untie yourself before we get home".

So home we made it and I gave her an emergency pill.

Keishawn at this point in her life is getting better, feeding herself but still required to wear diapers. Because of this new life, still we had to make changes like bells on her door and her room. When the bell on her door wasn't doing the job, I started thinking of safety so we resorted to a half door, cutting her room door in half. Finally I felt safe when I closed my eyes. Looking back I never in my wildest dreams imagined us being were we are. It was times like this I had to dig deep to make it thru to the next minute. As a child I always heard people say that God won't put more on you than you can bare. Honestly I believe He gives some of us a little more just to check to see were your faith really is. I remember in 2013 during the winter months sleeping (me and her) in the truck because it had a calming affect. I would come home from Williams Rd were I was working 2 shifts, eat, take a shower than me and her would head to the truck for bed. Now honestly I am not sure if she was sleeping because I was asleep. I just know she was quiet. We as mothers will do whatever we must for our children. This was very so for me. At times I would say Felecia, really in the car!, but it worked that's all I know! I must say even with a normal child what works for one household may not work for the next. Same being for someone that id disabled, it's simply trial and error what will or won't work? To you who may be reading this book, I say to you trials and tribulations may come but keep the faith, keep trusting in God.

Today is March 1, 2016 and my daughter has just had surgery. I was laying in the bed with her, just watching her rest. Resting is not something she can often do. Once I realized she had fallen asleep, it's time for me to get up to take on the duties around our home. When you want to provide better things for your family, then you make sacrifices and that's where I am, writing this book in hopes that one day, pen and paper will take me somewhere to help my family live better.

There are times that a mother will work with little to no sleep just to make that vision come true.

No matter, as I look at her sleep for a minute, I can't help but wonder how many children, how many adults have a mother, need a mother and she is no where to be found.

Why do some of have mother's that will give up their last, stay up for no special reason, simply just because they are a mother. Someone didn't get it from the start and I am not talking about when they were delivered or became pregnant. It started back before they were even thought about.

But at the same time we must remember sometimes, having the best teacher doesn't matter. Everyone that has prepared a meal can't necessarily cook. Everyone that is a teacher, should not teach, so with that being said, sometimes some may need some extra guidance to do the job called mothering.

Being a mother doesn't come with a manual. You may find some people that will say to do this or that, but being a mother is something that should come to a woman naturally. Being a mother requires having late night prayers as well as some tears and yes those sleep-ness nights. As I have watched many woman mothering their children, there is no perfect way, just remember to do your best.

1. When feeling weak; Isaiah 40 29 and 31.

2. When stressed out; Psalms 55 v 22 don't be troubled, you trust in God for he said come to me let me carry your heavy burdens and he shall give you rest.

3. When going thru trials and tribulation; 1 Peter 1-7 don't give up.

4. When you are tired; Matthew 11 v 28 God gives us strength.

5. For hope; Psalms 27 v 14 he has a plan and its perfect.

6. For his grace; Psalms 84 v 11 his grace is given freely.

7. For Peace; Psalms v 11 when the holy spirit controls our lives we can have peace.

Check out these other books by Felicia McCardy

DON'T STARE AT ME PLEASE

PARENTS LIKE ME

AVAILABLE VIA AMAZON.COM

A little about the author Felicia McCardy.

I had strong independent mother who defined being a true mother.

I grew up in Seffner FL.

My first choice of a career was an LPN but I settled for being an CNA due to being a young mother with Kieshawn. I lost my mother in 1988 lost my sister in 2012 lost a brother in 1992 . When I lost her it hurt really bad but it made me a stronger woman and also just watching her struggle and never giving up. I have 2 daughters, Keishawn and Hope . I named her Hope because I prayed and also hoped throughout my pregnancy she would be normal. I raised my nieces due to my sister's passing. I LOVE to help others. I used to do a food outreach every Wednesday until recently due to a schedule change.

My hobbies, I would say most definitely would be fishing all I need is 1 bite

and I can sit there all day and yes yard sales and flea markets.

My interest would be spending me with family and I love the Lord

he gives me strength from day today.

I don't know where I would be without knowing him!

www.ingramcontent.com/pod-product-compliance
Lightning Source LLC
Chambersburg PA
CBHW041234040426
42444CB00002B/164